As a Community we are called to share the .... the outworking of our charism and calling. One of the ways in which we do this is by publishing a number of series of booklets that explore our core teaching. These series include:

- Gold series: an expansion on our Rule of Life – the Community's core teaching.

- Green Series: a look at our influences, past and present – the things that have shaped us.

- Red series: an exploration of spiritual formation and disciplines – to provide some tools for the inner journey.

These booklets are a way of developing Community life, but also a way of sharing something of the wisdom gained on our journey with people beyond the Community.

The exploration of the inner journey before God is at the heart of who we are as a Community as, in gaining understanding of ourselves, we learn how better to live with others. This booklet is the cornerstone of our Gold series exploring our core teaching.

To put each booklet in context, they all begin with a summary of our Rule of Life, the questions at our heart, and the purpose and nature of Northumbria Community.

The three questions at our heart

Northumbria Community is the gift of God to those whose hearts are set on pilgrimage and whose lives are constantly being redefined and redirected by the living out of these three questions. Companions in Community are able to help each other keep these questions alive.

- Who is it that you seek?
- How then shall we live?
- How shall we sing the Lord's song in a strange land?

Our purpose

To embody a set of values, described in our Rule of Life of Availability and Vulnerability, which echoes, and points to, the life of Christ, and to support one another in our commitment to orientate ourselves toward this as a way for living. Knowing we have named and committed ourselves to this Rule **fosters perseverance.**

To hold the truth of the paradox of the Christian journey as being one taken alone/together. Each must take the journey alone. There is no substitute for leaning our own head on the breast of Christ and listening for heartbeat of God. There is no abdicating our own responsibility for our own life and no shortcuts for the work, struggle and intimacy of the cell of the heart before God. Yet, whilst on the journey, we are together. Others are headed in the same direction and come alongside to offer encouragement. Sometimes this encouragement is direct and verbal, sometimes it is through friendship, sometimes it comes through prayer support, and sometimes it is knowing that someone else is on a similar path through the wilderness of the inner exile. Knowing we are connected to others on the journey **fosters courage.**

To inspire each other to each be our own one-of-a-kind, God-designed selves. In a culture of celebrity, consumerism and hyper-productivity, the Northumbria Community strengthens people to be themselves. Knowing we are each accepted for who we are, and accepting others for who they are, **fosters authenticity.**

To encourage each other to live the questions at the heart of our journey alone/together. No one is going to give us the answer. No one is going to show us what living this way looks likes for each of us in our own contexts. We have to risk, experiment and make peace with mystery. Living with the questions and discerning how to live the Rule in our own context **fosters creativity.**

To be a sign that another way of living is possible. Even if people are not called to be Companions with us, the living witness of an alternative way gives refreshment to those, both within and without the Church, who see and need it. Knowing there are real choices around how to live and connect **fosters hope.**

Our nature

The renewal of the church will come from a new type of monasticism which only has in common with the old an uncompromising allegiance to the Sermon on the Mount. It is high time men and women banded together to do this.

Dietrich Bonhoeffer

Dynamic and erratic, spontaneous and radical, audacious and immature, committed if not altogether coherent, ecumenically open and often experimental, visible here and there, now and then, but unsettled institutionally. Almost monastic in nature but most of all enacting a fearful hope for human life in society.

William Stringfellow

The Northumbria Community occupies an interesting 'Third Space', which is not the long established denominations or their traditional monastic communities, and nor is it a newer form of church or newer 'new monastic' community. One of the gifts of the Northumbria Community to the body of Christ today is that it is rooted through its thirty years of exploration, and yet at the same time it is also still seen to be experimental and prophetic.

John Pritchard

Availability & Vulnerability

A way for living

The Rule of the Northumbria Community

Summary of our Rule of Life

This is the Rule we embrace. This is the Rule we will keep:

we say Yes to Availability;
we say Yes to Vulnerability.

We are called to be available to God and to others:

- Firstly to be available to God in the **cell** of our own heart when we can be turned towards Him, and seek His face;

- then to be available to others in a call to exercise **hospitality**, recognising that in welcoming others we honour and welcome the Christ Himself;

- then to be available to others through participation in His care and concern for them, by praying and **interceding** for their situations in the power of the Holy Spirit;

- then to be available for participation in **mission** of various kinds according to the calling and initiatives of the Spirit.

We are called to intentional, deliberate vunerability:

- We embrace the vulnerability of being **teachable** expressed in:

    - a discipline of prayer;
    - in exposure to Scripture;
    - a willingness to be accountable to others in ordering our ways and our heart in order to effect change.

- We embrace the responsibility of taking the **heretical imperative**:
    - by speaking out when necessary or asking awkward questions that will often upset the status quo;
    - by making relationships the priority, and not reputation.

- We embrace the challenge to live as church without walls, living openly amongst unbelievers and other believers in a way that the life of God in ours can be seen, challenged or questioned. This will involve us building friendships outside our Christian ghettos or club-mentality, not with ulterior evangelistic motives, but because we genuinely care.

This Rule is adhered to by all who are Companions in the Northumbria Community – a network of people, hugely diverse, from different backgrounds, streams and edges of the Christian faith, who are united in their desire to embrace and express an ongoing exploration into a new Way for Living that offers hope in the changed and changing culture of today's world.

The following introduction to the Rule has been written by Trevor Miller, one of the leaders of the Northumbria Community.

Introduction

A Rule of life is absolutely essential to any monastic life. It says 'this is who we are, this is our story'; and it reminds us of those things God has put on our hearts, calling us back to our foundations. The idea of a Rule of life developed in Christian monastic communities, and indeed, monasteries and convents today still function under a Rule, the best-known of which is that of St Benedict, dating from the 6th century. Monastic stability is based on accountability to the Rule of life; it serves as a framework for freedom – not as a set of rules that restrict or deny life, but as a way of living out our vocation alone and together. It is rooted in Scripture, pointing always to Christ; and, in the words of St Benedict, it is 'simply a handbook to make the very radical demands of the gospel a practical reality in daily life.'

> In the developing history of monasticism each community or monastic order has had its own particular areas of strength, calling and emphasis. One may be contemplative; another may have at its heart a calling to serve the poor; another the carrying of the Gospel to people of different languages or culture-groups; another may have its strengths in spiritual direction, education or discipleship. Their Rule will reflect this emphasis and provide a basic ground in the common calling of everyone identified as part of the community. When it became time to formulate our Community Rule we tried to discern what the vows should be which would reflect the character and spirituality of the Community as it had already developed. It was as a result of this reflection that Availability and Vulnerability were to be embraced as the distinctive charisms of our Community.
>
> *Andy Raine*

The history of the Northumbria Community is one of responding to a call we believe to be from God: a call to risky living, exploring 'a new monasticism' and our Rule developed out of this life already being lived. In effect it was a written response to the many people who were asking what was central to our hopes and dreams, and what were the values and emphases that reflected the character and ethos of our way for living. By a process of trial and error we found we were learning to live the questions as well as ask them: How then shall we live? Who is it that you seek? How shall we sing the Lord's song in a strange land? Living these questions, rather than providing pat answers that effectively ended the quest, actually became lifeblood for the Community. We discovered the reality of Rowan Williams' statement that 'Christ indeed answers our questions; but he also questions our answers.'

This is really important to understand: our Rule is **our response to these questions**. It is not an answer, only a response: an exploration of a way for living rooted in liberty rather than legalism or licence.

> For us, the life came before the Rule. We were living, hoping and dreaming these things before they were ever written down. So, we must focus not on the Rule, but on the things God has put on our heart. The Rule serves to remind us of these things, serves as a check, and calls us back to see if our dreams are still there. 'It has more to do with a spiritual vision of community life, with roots continually to be rediscovered, than with a legislation document' as *The Taizé Story* says in discussing their own community Rule.
>
> *Andy Raine*

A Rule then is a means whereby, under God, we take responsibility for the pattern of our spiritual lives. It is a 'measure' rather than a 'law'. The word 'rule' has bad connotations for many, implying restrictions, limitations and legalistic attitudes. But a Rule is essentially about **freedom.** It helps us to stay centred, bringing perspective and clarity to the way of life to which God has called us. The word derives from the Latin *regula* which means 'rhythm, regularity of pattern, a recognisable standard' for the conduct of life. Esther De Waal has pointed out that *regula* 'is a feminine noun which carried gentle connotations' rather than the harsh negatives that we often associate with the phrase 'rules and regulations' today. We do not want to be legalistic. A Rule is an orderly way of existence but we embrace it as a way of life not as keeping a list of rules. It is a means to an end – and the end is that we might seek God with authenticity and live more effectively for Him.

> Being bound to a Rule of life could be very restricting, but it is a voluntary and purposeful restriction. It excludes other possibilities in order to be focused on what is chosen. There are new and demanding priorities, but there is also much joy.
> *Andy Raine*

The word for Rule has a double root-meaning; one is that of a 'signpost' which has a purpose of pointing away from itself so as to inform the traveller that they are going in the right direction on their journey. It would be foolish to claim we have arrived if we are only at the signpost! We don't stop at the Rule and venerate it. The other root-meaning is that of 'a banister railing' which is something that gives support as you move forward, climbing or descending on your journey.

Why do we need a Rule?

The purpose of a Rule is to lay down working guidelines for the inner life and also provide a framework for the balanced ordering of work, leisure and social relationships. Hence a Rule of life is not only relevant to the monastic tradition: the principles can be used by anyone who is concerned about how they live their lives and they provide markers and guidelines, inspired by the Spirit, to help them on their journey towards God.

It becomes for us 'an exterior framework for an interior journey': a kind of scaffolding to use to build the spiritual structure of our individual life with God. It provides creative boundaries and spiritual disciplines whilst still leaving plenty of room for growth, development and flexibility. It is a railing to hold on to as we journey in our search for God, and, when we are blown off course, it is a signpost to a safe haven. It gives us a means of perception: a way of seeing so that we can attempt to handle our lives and relationships more wisely.

An illustration of the purpose of a Rule of life is to think of an analogy with our spectacles. We don't look **at** our glasses, however expensive or original they are. The reason why we don't look **at** them is that the whole purpose of having a pair of glasses is to look **through** their lenses to what we see in everyday life. It would be utter foolishness if all we did was to look at the glasses rather than look through them to what they revealed to us.

A Rule is meant to be a spur to growth. It can be likened to a stake used to hold up a plant. By providing structure and support to the plant, it enables the plant to grow quickly and healthily. In a similar way, a Rule of life provides structure and support not only to our prayer life, but to every aspect of life, enabling us to grow into the persons God wants us to be. Because of this, a Rule works best when it challenges us. It can't be so easy that we are not stretched: but neither can it be so demanding that we have difficulty even meeting its minimum standards. Otherwise it is likely to discourage us, and therefore to defeat its own purpose. A Rule is not there to make us feel good or feel bad, but to help our individual growth in spiritual maturity. If it becomes hard to follow, becomes a burden or causes you feelings of guilt, then give it up – it is not for you.

> A Rule must be appropriate. It must inspire a journey of exploration, aided by perceptive guidelines, themselves applicable to and interpretive of the real life of each traveller.
> *Alex Whitehead*

Just as we all have habits and routines that make our lives flow that much easier, so a Rule enables us to adopt a chosen daily pattern of life helping us on our faith journey to focus and refocus on God. It is a means of recollection in which we are constantly reminded of principles that further our seeking after God.

As a geographically-dispersed Community our Rule of life is deliberately flexible and adaptable, so that it does not **prescribe uniformly**, but **provokes individually**. It describes a process whereby we each seek God alone – whoever we are, wherever we are, whatever we are – so we can each be a sign of vulnerability, a sign of availability, wherever we are as a scattered Community. Yet at the same time our life together is intentional: it is not a haphazard, 'anything-goes' individual interpretation. We do have a common purpose and for that reason our Rule of life is a statement reflecting our shared understanding of the principles of our life and what is necessary to maintain it. The Rule is a living instrument; a source of inspiration; and a subject of constant study, reflection and prayer. Its value and power depend on its ability to act as a lens through which we can interpret life as we experience it and as God currently leads us.

We don't want to box God into denominations or narrow statements of faith – we've seen the damage these can do. Those who feel it is of vital importance to hold a 'pre-millennial, post-tribulationist position within a dispensationalist view of the Second Coming of Christ" will struggle with our deliberately flexible and adaptable Rule of Life!

We don't want uniformity; we don't want to become 'established'; and we don't want to conform tidily. We want to remain raw and ragged – because we are not a commodity to be packaged, as it were, so that somebody can say, 'I've read your bumph, been there, done that, where's the T-shirt?'

We want to emphasise that our Rule does not **prescribe**: it **provokes**. It is descriptive rather than prescriptive – the very opposite of a uniform approach. In effect, it is saying, bring all your idiosyncrasies, prejudices and crap, all your unique experience, all your knowledge and understanding of life – bring it all to the Rule of Availability and Vulnerability. We must then learn to hold it loosely so as to make our own discoveries, coming to the realisation that there won't always be an answer and that it's OK to keep living those questions: How then shall we live? Who is God? Who am I? What is real?

This will lead us to a further realisation that God gives different answers to different people in different situations and circumstances. In many ways it would be so much easier to say, 'Do this', 'Don't do that', 'Say three Hail Marys', 'Say two Our Fathers four times a day'; but we need broad strokes and general principles to which we can each apply our specifics – our own unique set of circumstances and relationships.

> A Rule offers 'creative boundaries within which God's loving presence can be recognised and celebrated.' It does not prescribe but invite, it does not force but guide, it does not threaten but warn, it does not instil fear but points to love. In this it is a call to freedom, freedom to love.
>
> *Henri Nouwen*

Life should have large elements of spontaneity and our approach to it should be infinitely adaptable. But the Rule provides key markers, some of which will just be temporary check-points, but others will be relevant throughout our whole lives.

How do we use a Rule as a way for living?

A monastic rule not only underpins the corporate life of a community; it also provides the model for an individual Rule outside the cloister. Basically, an individual Rule consists of a set of established agreements made by an individual as promises to God regarding spiritual practice. Thus to adopt a Rule of life is to provide a structure for one's own spiritual journey; and a good first step to take is to find a soulfriend or spiritual director who can help us apply the Rule realistically to our own individual circumstances.

A contemporary Rule must wrestle with daily life, being applicable to the good, the bad and the ugly elements in all our lives. It is not a technique or a spiritual diet but a framework that helps us step by step and in a natural way, to incorporate reminders of God's presence into the life we already live. Repetition and association are key elements in sustaining a spiritual life. The human spirit requires ritual. The stories we tell, the myths that shape us and give us meaning, need to be acted out. A Rule creates a structure in which we can recall God's presence by associating that presence with common, daily things. It provides a rhythm of remembrance – punctuating our day with opportunities to refocus on God. It enables us to redeem the daily round of life – not by escaping it, but by finding the holy in the ordinary. Otherwise we will spend our lives discovering again and again the folly of believing the grass is always greener on the other side.

A Rule of life helps us to stay connected to God in the present moment by noticing the now – not by adding disciplines to an already busy life but by becoming conscious of God in what we are already doing. Our part is to remain available, to listen, to observe, to act, to be. This enables us to remain spiritually alive – mindful of God's presence with us. Mindfulness is to be aware of what is going on. Live in the 'now': life is just the next thing that happens. The present is where we always are. 'Yesterday's the past, tomorrow's the future, but today is a gift. That's why it is called the present.'

United by our Rule

Our Rule expresses a spirituality that is grounded, coming out of the hard-won experience and chaos of those who have faced some of the hard questions: How do I live with myself? How do I live with others? How do I relate to the world around me? How do I find time and space for God?

Paradoxically the Rule will send us in two directions – inward into the heart of God and on the outward journey of service in the world. Cultivating these spiritual disciplines will create the freedom to love, and enable the spiritual life to become visible. This will in turn create the space where God's love and grace can reach us, heal us, direct us and free us to be the persons we truly are.

Our Rule is a Way for Living as 'internal emigrés' in the current cultural climate. First of all, we are called to **Availability**: to God in the cell of our own heart where we can seek Him for His own sake, as the 'one thing necessary.' Then to be available to others in a call to exercise hospitality, recognising that in welcoming others we honour and welcome Christ Himself. We are then called to be available to others through participation in God's care and concern for them by praying and interceding for their situations in the power of His Holy Spirit. We are also called to be available for mission of various kinds according to the leading and initiatives of the Spirit. Then as our Rule is an ongoing exploration of 'How then shall we live?' it also involves an intentional **Vulnerability** expressed through being teachable in the discipline of prayer; through applying the wisdom of the Scriptures; and through a mutual accountability in the advocacy of soul friends. Also we live the vulnerability of embracing the 'heretical imperative' by challenging assumed truth; being receptive to constructive criticism; affirming that relationship matters more than reputation and by living openly among people as 'Church without walls.'

Conclusion

This is a way for living we share even though we are scattered widely in a geographic sense. Remember we are not a residential Community but a Community of the heart. We are not a Community because of physically living close to each other (although some do) but because we live close to our chosen way of living and the vow we have all taken to be Available and Vulnerable as outlined in our Rule.

> These people have been called together to be a sign and a witness, to accomplish a particular mission, which is their charism, their gift.
>
> *Jean Vanier*

> We are to be a sign of vulnerability, a sign of availability, wherever we are as a scattered and dispersed Community. The Rule is a way of living out our salvation together. It reminds us of ways to live that make sense, and are in accordance with Scripture, in accordance with the ways of God and are appropriate to our task or vocation. The Rule has become our story. It is a story that needs to be lived in. It is a story that needs to be lived out, not just talked about. The Rule continues to challenge our hearts and lives, as it is immediately relevant to real living. It addresses honest questions, and touches on issues with which most of us have wrestled in various forms for many years. Through the Rule comes the gentle but insistent call of Jesus to follow Him closely.
>
> *Andy Raine*

Our calling as Christians is to be Christ-like – to be conformed to His image (see 2 Corinthians 3:18). The heart of every Rule of life, and applicable to all Christians, is the gospel of Jesus Christ. He is the Way, the Truth, the Life. The goal of the Christian life is love – for God, for our neighbour, for self, for others. We are a pilgrim people on a journey of faith. As a Community we are bound together in a common vocation: to seek God and know self so as to better live with others and serve the world of our influence be it great or small.

Availability to God and others

- **The cell**

'We are called to be available to God and to others in the cell of our own heart when we can be turned towards Him, and seek His face...'

> The Cry to God as 'Father'
> in the New Testament
> is not a calm acknowledgement
> of a universal truth
> about God's abstract fatherhood.
> It is the child's cry
> out of a nightmare.
>
> It is the cry of outrage,
> fear, shrinking away,
> when faced with
> the horror of the 'world'–
> yet not simply or exclusively protest,
> but trust as well.
>
> 'Abba, Father'
> all things are possible
> to Thee.
>
> *Rowan Williams*

> It is always much more
> difficult to sing when
> the audience has turned
> its back
>
> *Calvin Miller*

Seek God for yourself:
don't get others to do it for you

John Skinner

The cell is not something you do –
it's something it does to you that makes the difference.
It's a death, a willingness to be unknown.

John Skinner

Know yourself and you will find your right seat.

I have prepared a place for you,
says the Lord, that is for you,
and only you, to fill.
First of all, come to My table,
and ask that you might serve,
looking even for the lowest tasks.
When the work of service is done
then you may look for your own place at table.
But do not seek the most important place
in case it is reserved for someone else.
The place I have appointed is where you will be happiest.

Andy Raine

When someone invites you to a wedding feast, do not take the place of honour, for a person more distinguished than you may have been invited. If so, the host who invited both of you will come and say to you, 'Give this man your seat'. Then, humiliated, you will have to take the least important place. But when you are invited, take the lowest place, so that when your host comes, he will say to you, 'Friend, move up to a better place'. Then you will be honoured in the presence of all your fellow guests.

For everyone who exalts himself will be humbled, and he who humbles himself will be exalted.

Luke 14:8–11

Take me often from the tumult of things
into Thy presence.
There show me what I am
and what Thou hast purposed me to be.
Then hide me from Thy tears.

Hebridean Altars

• Hospitality

'We are called ... to be available to others in a call to exercise hospitality, recognising that in welcoming others we honour and welcome the Christ Himself...'

Celtic Rune of Hospitality

I saw a stranger yestere'en.
I put food in the eating place,
drink in the drinking place,
music in the listening place,
and in the sacred name of the Triune
He blessed myself and my house,
my cattle and my dear ones,
and the lark said in her song
often, often, often,
goes Christ in the stranger's guise.

Kenneth MacLeod

Brigid's Feast

I should welcome the poor to my feast,
for they are God's children.
I should welcome the sick to my feast,
for they are God's joy.
Let the poor sit with Jesus at the highest place,
and the sick dance with the angels.

Celtic Fire

The Great Banquet Table

> In the middle of the street appeared a great banquet table, laden with all kinds of food. And coming to be seated at the table were the poor, the sick, the hungry, the old, the young, the rejected, the disabled. And serving them at the table was none other than the Man of Sorrows himself. He was gathering a large group of men and women to help him. Some of them I recognised. They were friends of mine who had left the mountain to come down here and work. They seemed happier here, somehow, than up there in their homes on the mountain. They seemed full of purpose. They seemed full of a strange kind of joy that ran deep, even though I saw that many had learned to weep, perhaps for the first time. Some were tending to the sick, some were building shelters; all would come to listen to the Man of Sorrows, who spoke to them and taught them. Some were being sent to the walls that held back the waters, to dig beneath the walls and set free the waters of the river once more to run through the city to provide life and beauty for all. And they sang as they worked.
>
> Ken Medema A Place for Dreaming

• Praying and interceding

'We are called ... to be available to others through participation in His care and concern for them, by praying and interceding for their situations in the power of the Holy Spirit...'

> Those who lean on Jesus' breast feel the heart-beat of God.
> Monk of Patmos

> Now there was leaning on Jesus' breast one of his disciples, whom Jesus loved.
> John 13:23

> Surely the Sovereign Lord does nothing without revealing his plan to His servants the prophets.
> Amos 3:7

> Mary, his mother, kept all these things and sayings and pondered on them in her own heart.
>
> *Luke 2:51b*

> God shares His secrets with those who keep them.
>
> *Joy Dawson*

> So Joshua fought the Amalekites as Moses had ordered, and Moses, Aaron and Hur went to the top of the hill. As long as Moses held up his hands, the Israelites were winning, but whenever he lowered his hands, the Amalekites were winning. When Moses' hands grew tired, they took a stone and put it under him and he sat on it. Aaron and Hur held his hands up – one at one side, one on the other – so that his hands remained steady till sunset. So Joshua overcame the Amalekite army with the sword.
>
> *Exodus 17:10-13*

• Mission

'We are called ... to be available for participation in mission of various kinds according to the calling and initiatives of the Spirit...'

> As the tide draws the waters
> close in upon the shore,
> make me an island,
> set apart,
> alone with you, God,
> holy to you.
>
> Then with the turning of the tide
> prepare me to carry your presence
> to the busy world that rushes in on me
> till the waters come again
> and fold me back to you.

Mission starts at home; continues outside the home with whoever we meet; but may also involve making a journey to be in the right place to be used by God at the Spirit's initiative.

- **The tide is in – at home**

   Within the home we should ideally see a microcosm of the monastery.
   We should seek to be freeing each other for the love of God.
   We must be valuing each person.
   Family life is holy ground.

   John Skinner

   It is ordinary life that counts: there must be no discrepancy between what I claim to believe and how I live.

   Andy Raine

- **The tide is out – outside the home**

   As Aidan walked along he stopped and spoke to whoever he met, both rich and poor: if they were heathen, he invited them to embrace the mystery of the faith, and be baptised; and if they were already believers, he strengthened their faith, inspiring them by word and action to be good and generous to their neighbours.

   Bede

- **The coracle is on the sea – 'Peregrinati' or 'Obedience without an agenda'**

Sometimes we will be called to be **peregrinati** – those who set out from home as His journeyers – travellers for the love of Christ. (The word 'peregrinati' comes from the Latin *pro christo peregrinati volens* which means 'willing to set out and journey for love of Christ'.)

> No peregrinati journey should ever be undertaken begrudgingly but instead with love and thankfulness, saying, 'I thank You for this, my God. I am a traveller and stranger in the world, like so many of Your people before me.'
>
> *St Columba*

There is a characteristic theme which recurs in the story of the Celtic saints. It is of the wanderer who sets out, like Abraham, at the initiative of the Holy Spirit without fully realising what this is all about or where in detail he may be going – or even whether he will return. It is a sense of adventure, of openness to possibilities, abandonment to God, and expectation of fulfilling His will. We are called in a similar way to accept responsibility for our choices in this area, and hope that it is the voice of the Holy Spirit we have heard. **It is a call to risky living.**

> By faith Abraham, when called to go to a place he would later receive as his inheritance, obeyed and went, even though he did not know where he was going. By faith he made his home in the promised land like a stranger in a foreign country; he lived in tents, as did Isaac and Jacob, who were heirs with him of the same promise. For he was looking forward to the city with foundations, whose architect and builder is God.
>
> *Hebrews 11:8–10*

> Now an angel of the Lord said to Philip, 'Go south to the road – the desert road – that goes down from Jerusalem to Gaza.' So he started out, and on his way he met an Ethiopian eunuch, an important official in charge of all the treasury of Candace, queen of the Ethiopians. This man had gone to Jerusalem to worship, and on his way home was sitting in his chariot reading the book of Isaiah the prophet. The Spirit told Philip, 'Go to the chariot and stay near it'. Then Philip ran up to the chariot and heard the man reading Isaiah the prophet. 'Do you understand what you are reading?' Philip asked. 'How can I', he said, 'unless someone explains it to me?' So he invited Philip to come up and sit with him. The eunuch was reading this passage of Scripture:

> He was led like a sheep to the slaughter, and as a lamb before the sheerer is silent, so he did not open his mouth. In his humiliation he was deprived of justice. Who can speak for his defendants? For his life was taken from the earth.
>
> The eunuch asked Philip, 'Tell me, please, who is the prophet talking about, himself or someone else?' Then Philip began with that very passage out of Scripture and told him the good news about Jesus. As they travelled along the road, they came to some water and the eunuch said, 'Look, here is water. Why shouldn't I be baptised?' And he gave orders to stop the chariot. Then both Philip and the eunuch went down into the water and Philip baptised him. When they came up out of the water the Spirit of the Lord suddenly took Philip away, and the eunuch did not see him again, but went on his way rejoicing. Philip, however, appeared at Azotus and travelled about, preaching the gospel in all the towns until he reached Caesarea.

Acts 8:26-40

Rhymes from a Lindisfarne Monk

He is my King
In my heart He's hid
He is my joy all joys amid
I am a drop in His ocean lost
His coracle I, on His wide sea tossed
A leaf in His storm
The book of His praise
In my wallet slung
The cloak of His friendship round me flung
Hither and thither about I'm blown
My way an eddy, my rest a stone
And He my fire

Marjorie Milne

Intentional vulnerability

Vulnerable: open enough to be hurt, not given to self-defence.

- Teachableness

'We are called to intentional deliberate vulnerability. We embrace the vulnerability of being teachable expressed in...'

- a discipline of prayer

A daily discipline of prayer is important. It is often inconvenient and may be dry, but gives stability to our life, making prayer its foundation, and allowing God to teach us inwardly.

The Office is there to serve us in this capacity, and it is recommended that Companions in Community use this as an expression of our common life in God.

- exposure to Scripture

> The Scriptures are our memory-book.
> *John Skinner*

> I have to be right before God and I have to read my Bible and stay informed on who we are, and who God is.
> *Larry Norman*

> Your word is a lamp to my feet and a light for my path.
> *Psalm 119:105*

As we keep allowing Scripture to confront our experience it will direct our paths.

Andy Raine

- a willingness to be accountable to others in ordering our ways and our heart in order to effect change.

A teachable spirit is to be cultivated as well as chosen. It doesn't happen overnight. We voluntarily allow someone to have the right to speak into our life (or into some area of our life). We are prepared to listen to the wisdom and experience of that individual and of the church.

> We learn of course, from one another – as collective wisdom and life's experience are good teachers. And there has to be accountability in all relationships through mutual respect and sensitivity; but as we are all blind to our own failings and often build defences around our fragile egos, it sometimes helps to have another person whose walk with God we respect sharing our inner journey. Someone who accepts us as we are, and who, through their own vulnerability, is honest enough yet gentle enough to help us discern our motives and actions.
>
> *Trevor Miller*

- ### The heretical imperative

'We are called to ... embrace the responsibility of taking the heretical imperative...'

> Anything is called 'heretical' that challenges the assumed understanding of what is the truth. In time, the status quo is equated in people's thinking with the truth – but truth is alive and active, more powerful than any two-edged sword.

An 'imperative' is an order – it merely tells us that we **must**. So by definition the 'heretical imperative' is the necessity to risk misunderstanding or charges of heresy in the pursuit and exposition of truth. This is an extremely **vulnerable** occupation.

Obedience to the heretical imperative is not being afraid to listen, to ask questions, to be converted to truth in whatever form it may be presented. There is often more truth to be found expressed in secular, or non-Christian, statements that are genuinely concerned about, for example, areas of injustice – than in rehearsals of 'the true' in Christian language, when they are concerned merely with maintaining the status quo.

Andy Raine and John Skinner

It is a seeking of wisdom, which is knowledge honed by experience. A good example of this is the story of Bonhoeffer and his close friend Eberhard Bethge sitting in a café garden when a news bulletin preceded by the usual blasts of trumpets came over the radio. All the customers leaped to their feet to give the Heil Hitler salute, and burst into the Horst Wessel song. Bonhoeffer rose with them, gave the salute and joined in the singing, hissing at the astonished Bethge to do likewise. **'There's a time to stand and a time to sit. A mere salute is not worth dying for'** he explained. He had greater things to do than risk being imprisoned for a foolhardy expression of support.

Trevor Miller

- by speaking out when necessary or asking awkward questions that will often upset the status quo

Before you are able to convince me of error you must first demonstrate you understand what I say!

Charles Finney

> Christians constantly warn other believers to keep away from those they consider dangerous by saying, 'Don't have anything to do with them – they're in error!' If the Holy Spirit is to lead us into all truth, have you got there yet? **No!** And if you're not in all truth what are you in?
>
> The question is: How **much** in error are you?
>
> *Arthur Burt*

Criticism is useful in the Community. It cannot be given with bitterness. It cannot be expressed in insults, in acts or judgements that offend the honour of individuals or groups. It should avoid recourse to inappropriate forms of publicity.

If it comes from the Holy Spirit, criticism must be animated by the desire to advance in truth and love. It must be filled with respect, always adhering to the directions given by the Lord about correcting another: 'If your brother sins against you, go and show him his fault, just between the two of you. If he listens to you, you have won your brother over. But if he will not listen, take two others along, so that every matter may be established by the testimony of two or three witnesses.' (Matthew 18:15–16) The Community must always be reformed, and try to correct its imperfections. Criticism can often help the Community to take a new step forward.

It appears from the history of the Church, and particularly from the lives of the saints, that frequently the Holy Spirit inspires prophetic words meant to foster the development or the reform of the Christian community's life. Sometimes these words are addressed especially to those who wield authority.

There are many faithful and, above all, many saints who have given popes and other pastors of the Church the light and strength necessary for fulfilling their mission, especially at difficult times for the Church. This fact shows the possibility and usefulness of freedom of speech in the Church: a freedom that can also appear in the form of constructive criticism. The important thing is that what is said truly expresses a prophetic inspiration coming from the Spirit. As St Paul says, 'Where the Spirit of the Lord is, there is freedom.' (2 Corinthians 3:17)

The Holy Spirit fosters sincerity between us and a mutual trust.

> I myself am convinced that you yourselves are full of goodness, complete in knowledge and competent to instruct one another.
>
> *Romans 15:14*

> For by Him all things were created: things in heaven and on earth, visible and invisible, whether thrones or powers or rulers or authorities; all things were created by Him and for Him.
>
> *Colossians 1:16*

> Therefore each of you must put off falsehood and speak truthfully to his neighbour, for we are all members of one body.
>
> *Ephesians 4:25*

• by making relationships the priority, and not reputation

Jesus was prepared to make friends with people who were marginalised in the society of his day, and to risk misunderstanding in the process. We should do the same, and also cover one another in love as much as we are able.

Juan Carlos Ortiz tells of a brother who was in ministry with him, but fell into sin. At first the other leaders wanted to distance themselves (and the church) from him quickly Then they realised that when he had been a success they were quick to own his achievements as an extension of their own – now they should be identified with his failure also, and seek to see him restored.

Church without walls

'We are called to ... embrace the challenge to live as church without walls, living openly amongst unbelievers in a way that the life of God in ours can be seen, challenged or questioned. This will involve us building friendships outside our Christian ghettos or club-mentality, not with ulterior evangelistic motives, but because we genuinely care.'

Kingdom in the Streets.

> Come walk with me in the darkness,
> and as we walk along,
> I'll tell you quite a story,
> and I'll sing you quite a song.
> I'll sing of light and darkness,
> of victory and defeat,
> corruption on the mountains
> and compassion in the street.
>
> We're walking to the city,
> and Chaos is its name,
> and in its streets and alleys
> are the blind, the sick, the maimed.
> And the children cry for water,
> and relief seems out of sight,
> and they dream about tomorrow
> in the darkness of the night.
>
> For it's a long night,
> and weary grow the feet
> that walk the long road,
> but the morning will come sweet.
> Yes, it's a long night,
> and the Prince is in the streets tonight.
>
> Well, just outside that city,
> far from the blight and pain,

is a holy mountain fortress
where life seems calm and sane.
There's feasting there and singing
by tranquil waterfalls,
and the street folks never come there
'cause they cannot CLIMB the WALLS.

At the gateway to the fortress
the Man of Sorrows cries –
a Prince in beggar's clothing
with compassion in His eyes.
And the mountain folk won't hear Him,
so He turns his feet around,
and the ruler of the mountains
becomes a servant in the town.

I see His Kingdom coming,
I see the victory day.
There'll be no need of fortress walls,
for there is a better way.

The Prince will lift the lowly,
and the proud will taste defeat –
don't look for the Kingdom on the mountain,
for it's coming in the streets.

Ken Medema

Don't build walls for the non-Christian to climb over.

This conversion business becomes a higher and higher wall that they must climb over; Christians, in reinforcing their arguments, have unconsciously built it so high that their non-Christian friends doubt they have the strength or desire to get over it to the other side.

Yet it is the Christians who can reach through the wall and be with their friends, if they dare.

A lot of good sharing of experience just doesn't happen – simply because Christians develop an attitude of 'Oh, but you wouldn't understand that.' Non-Christians are not creatures of some lesser or different species, but people with one sense not yet developed, their spirits dormant like a balloon waiting to be filled with the breath of God. Their other senses may well be utilised more fully and properly than the Christian's – they may be more diligent and earnest in their pursuit of truth, or more compassionate and self-sacrificing.

> Don't have ulterior motives.

We must be prepared to love someone as they are, not in the hope that eventually they will become a Christian.

> **The choice is ours to come out from behind the walls and make friends with those around us.**

If the life in us is genuine, it will affect those about us, not in any self-conscious way, but as salt flavours everything. We must care, not with any ulterior evangelistic motive, but as an expression of our identity in God if indeed it is genuine.

> **If the church walls come down we will be known for who we are, and if that is not the presence of Christ to all around, then it is time we got sorted out so it can be.**

>> Don't look for the Kingdom on the mountains,
>> for it's coming in the streets.
>>
>> *Ken Medema*

Declaration of Faith

There is no other God,
there never was
and there never will be,
than God the Father,
unbegotten and without beginning,
the Lord of the Universe,
as we have been taught,
and His son Jesus Christ
whom we declare to have
always been with the Father
and to have been begotten
spiritually by the Father,
in a way that baffles description,
before the beginning of the world,
before all beginning;
and by Him are made
all things visible and invisible.

He was made man,
defeated death,
and was received into heaven
by the Father,
who has given Him power
over all names in heaven,
on earth, and under the earth;
and every tongue
will acknowledge to Him
that Jesus Christ is the Lord God.

We believe in Him
and we look for His coming soon
as judge of the living and the dead
who will treat everyone according to their deeds.

He has poured out
the Holy Spirit
upon us in abundance,
the gift and guarantee of eternal life
who makes those who believe and obey
children of God
and joint heirs with Christ.

We acknowledge and adore Him
as one God in the Trinity
of the holy name.

St Patrick

The Rule of the Northumbria Community

Availability to God and others:

- Cell
- Hospitality
- Intercession
- Mission

Intentional vulnerability:

- Teachableness:
    - prayer
    - Scripture as memory-book
    - accountability

- Heretical imperative:
    - constructive criticism
    - relationship not reputation
    - church without walls

For more information about the Northumbria Community please contact:

Northumbria Community
Nether Springs
Croft Cottage
Acton Home Farm
Felton
Northumberland
NE65 9NU

office@northumbriacommunity.org

+44 (0)1670 787645

www.northumbriacommunity.org

To see our resources including *Celtic Daily Prayer*, published by Collins and now available in two volumes:

Celtic Daily Prayer Book 1: The Journey Begins
ISBN 9780008123024

and

Celtic Daily Prayer Book 2: Farther Up and Farther In
ISBN 9780008100193

please visit our online shop:

www.northumbriacommunity.org/shop

© The Northumbria Community Trust
Registered Charity Number: 1156630